WHEN

I

CAN'T

Maria Boyd

WestBow Press books may be ordered through booksellers or by contacting:

WestBow Press
A Division of Thomas Nelson & Zondervan
1663 Liberty Drive
Bloomington, IN 47403
www.westbowpress.com
844-714-3454

All Scripture quotations are taken from The Holy Bible, New International Version®, NIV® Copyright © 1973, 1978, 1984, 2011 by Biblica, Inc.® Used by permission. All rights reserved worldwide.

ISBN: 978-1-6642-6408-3 (sc)
ISBN: 978-1-6642-6409-0 (e)

Library of Congress Control Number: 2022907575

Print information available on the last page.

WestBow Press rev. date: 08/22/2022

WESTBOW
PRESS®
A DIVISION OF THOMAS NELSON
& ZONDERVAN

WHEN I

I

CAN'T

When it feels like you CAN'T

Remember...

I CAN

Do ALL things

Through CHRIST

Which Strengthens Me

"I Can Do All Things
Through Christ
Who Strengthens Me"
(Philippians 4:13)

Philippians 4:13

Printed in the United States
by Baker & Taylor Publisher Services